c.1117
...grove Priory is founded by Robert de la Haye, with a
...munity of Benedictine monks from the Abbey of Lessay
...Normandy

1269
...nciscan (Greyfriar) friars begin building a monastery in
...chester. Part of this building still remains and is now
...wn as the Guildhall

1348
...Black Death hits Sussex. Chichester's population is
...uced by up to a third

1500
...chester's well established needlemaking industry
...minates the English market throughout the 1500s

1520
...k starts on the new Cowdray House

1614
...e industrial ironworks make cannons and tools at
...nhurst Furnace, which operates for over 150 years

1664
...city of Chichester closes its gates against the spread of
...Great Plague

1749
...and hanging of several smugglers from the Hawkshurst
...g. Their bodies are hung in gibbets across the district as
...arning to other smugglers

1804
...am Blake is put on trial for sedition in Chichester
...dhall. He is accused of damning King George III but is
...uitted

1861
...Cathedral spire collapses. It has been unstable and
...cking for several months. Fortunately no one is injured
...a fundraising appeal for a new spire begins immediately

1892
...opam's, pioneers of canning meats and preserving food,
...ns a factory in East Street

1917
...Tangmere is founded and later becomes a key base
...ng the Battle of Britain

1962
...chester Festival Theatre opens with Laurence Olivier as
...first Artistic Director

1974
...avations of the bath house take place 1973–74

2011
...th Downs National Park becomes fully operational

2015
...chester-born astronaunt Tim Peake becomes the first
...sh ESA astronaut to visit the International Space Station

AD 10...
The bis...
cathedr...
and gro...
happeni...

AD 118...
The new...
by fire fo... ...ing the first fire in 1114

AD 1284
The first Coudreye House is built. It is later rebuilt as the
elaborate Tudor Cowdray House

AD 1400
A sturdy bell tower is built beside the Cathedral to house the
heavy bells

AD 1501
The Market Cross is built in Chichester as a gift from Bishop
Storey. People can now have market stalls and sell their
goods without getting rained on

AD 1526
Henry VIII stays at Petworth House on a hunting trip

AD 1642
The Siege of Chichester during the English Civil War. The
Parliamentarian General William Waller captures the city after
eight days

AD 1697
Goodwood House is bought by the 1st Duke of Richmond
and used as a country retreat

AD 1791
The last needlemaker in Chichester, William Scale, dies,
marking the end of the local needlemaking tradition

AD 1852
'Shadow' Mason is the last man to be punished using the
mobile stocks. He is sentenced to a humiliating two hours in
the stocks at the Market Cross

AD 1890
Ebenezer Prior buys the site now occupied by the
Novium Museum on Tower Street for a new woolstapling
establishment

AD 1897
The Hundred of Manhood and Selsey Tramway opens
between Selsey and Chichester

AD 1942
Tragedy at Petworth Boys' School when a bomb drops and
explodes in their Year 4 classroom, killing eight pupils and
two teachers

AD 1964
Chichester Harbour is designated an Area of Outstanding
Natural Beauty

AD 1990
Chichester Livestock Market closes

AD 2012
The Novium Museum opens to act as the official custodian of
Chichester District's heritage

Hello, and welcome to Chichester.

I was born and went to school here in this beautiful and historic city. I hope you will enjoy your visit and experience many of Chichester's outstanding historic attractions and cultural venues.

With best wishes,

Tim Peake

ABOVE Tim Peake, the first British ESA astronaut, launched into space on 15 December 2015 and returned to Earth on 18 June 2016.

ABOVE RIGHT Chichester Cathedral seen from Bishop's Palace Gardens.

Chichester nestles just inland from the clear blue sea of the popular Witterings beaches and Chichester Harbour, a designated Area of Outstanding Natural Beauty and one of the few remaining relatively wild and undeveloped coastal areas along the bustling South Coast. Further north, the chalk hills of the South Downs National Park encompass both fertile farmland and ancient woodland, providing diverse habitats. Chichester District, once used as ancient man's hunting ground and later a site of military invasion, now continues to draw sailors, walkers and creatives alike to experience its rich heritage and beautiful countryside.

Chichester was first established as *Noviomagus Reginorum*, which translates as the 'new market of

The History of
CHICHESTER

the proud people', after the Roman invasion in AD 43. This legacy can be found across the city, through the circuit of Roman walls that encircle the four main streets. North, South, East and West Streets run from the cardinal points of the Market Cross, and the remains of a Roman bath house, which are located inside the Novium Museum. Archaeological evidence points to the Roman town having been established sometime in the latter half of the first century AD. The town was later walled at the end of the third century. After the Romans abandoned the site, it was inhabited by Saxons in the latter half of the 5th century. It was at this time that the city got its name, from Cissa, son of the Anglo-Saxon King, and Old English *ceaster*, meaning 'Roman fort'.

The Normans transferred the seat of the local bishop from the traditional site at Selsey to Chichester in 1075; the following year, work began on a new cathedral, which has dominated the city ever since.

Chichester is now a city offering something for everyone. Locals continue to celebrate traditional fairs and festivals, such as the annual Sloe Fair, first held in Chichester over 900 years ago, and the Ebernoe Horn Fair. More recently, the Goodwood Festival of Speed and the New Year's Day Big Dip at East Wittering beach have become popular annual events.

We welcome you to Chichester and hope this guide will enable you to get the most out of your visit to this unique and historic Cathedral city.

Tower Street

THE NOVIUM MUSEUM AND CHICHESTER TOURIST INFORMATION CENTRE

The Novium Museum in Tower Street is the perfect place to start your exploration of this beautiful and fascinating city. Purpose-built in 2012 over the remains of Chichester's Roman bath house, this multi-award-winning modern museum tells the fascinating story of the history of the city and wider District, spanning more than 500,000 years, from the Paleolithic Boxgrove man to the present day. As custodians of the heritage of the Chichester District, the Novium Museum cares for a unique collection of over 500,000 objects, covering social history, archaeology, geology, photographs and a small art collection. The museum hosts an exciting programme of temporary exhibitions covering a broad range of subjects, so there's always something new to see when you visit.

ABOVE LEFT The Novium Museum opened in July 2012 and is built over the remains of the Roman bath house

ABOVE Chichester's iconic, Grade II listed circular library

LEFT New and old: looking down Tower Street with a view of the Novium Museum and Chichester Cathedral

CHICHESTER LIBRARY

There is an active programme of annual events, including Chichester Roman Week, which is held annually in May half term and features talks, heritage trails, guided tours and family activities. Admission to the museum is free but donations to support its upkeep are welcome. The Novium Museum also houses Chichester's Tourist Information Centre, where knowledgeable staff are on hand to help you make the most of your visit. Guided city walks and other excursions can be booked here.

A café overlooks the exposed Roman bath house so you can enjoy some refreshments whilst soaking in a view of more than 2,000 years of history. A well stocked gift shop is the perfect place to buy gifts and souvenirs.

Opposite the Novium Museum is the public library, which was built in 1967 and, at that time, was one of the most modern libraries in the world. Librarians came to Chichester from all over the globe to study its design. The library was awarded listed Grade II listed status in 2015 after being recognised for its architectural and historic interest. English Heritage deemed the library of 'national importance' and an 'exemplar from this period of library building'.

The circular design is described by the county architect F.R. Steele as having 'understated elegance both in its careful detailing and unbroken rhythm of its exterior and in the sculptural quality of its interior spaces'.

West Street

CHICHESTER CATHEDRAL

A stone's throw from the Novium Museum, and dominating West Street, you will find Chichester Cathedral.

For more than 900 years this magnificent cathedral has stood at the heart of Chichester. Site of the sacred Shrine of St Richard, this cathedral is both ancient and modern, with original medieval features sitting alongside world-famous contemporary artworks. Chichester Cathedral is renowned for its art, which includes paintings, tapestries, sculptures and stained glass. Contemporary works by acclaimed artists such as John Piper, Graham Sutherland, Marc Chagall and Philip Jackson complement paintings and carvings from every century since the cathedral's foundation.

The cathedral's detached bell tower was added in the 15th century. Housing a peal of eight bells, it is the only one of its kind remaining in England.

One of the cathedral's best known interior features is the Arundel Tomb. Immortalised in Philip Larkin's 1956 poem 'An Arundel Tomb', the tomb in the north aisle was brought from Lewes Priory after its dissolution in 1537. It is a tomb chest and on top lies the recumbent figures of Richard Fitzalan, earl of Arundel and his second wife, Eleanor of Lancaster. Larkin draws inspiration from this scene to muse on time, mortality and the nature of earthly love.

It begins:

Side by side, their faces blurred,
The earl and countess lie in stone,

ABOVE Bishop's Palace Gardens, a hidden treasure in the heart of Chichester, boasts a wealth of native flora and an arboretum with rare specimen trees

LEFT A peaceful afternoon in Bishop's Palace Gardens, with a view of the pergola walk and Chichester Cathedral

FAR LEFT Chichester Cathedral is famed for its spire, separate bell tower and acclaimed artwork spanning centuries

and concludes:

> Our almost-instinct almost true:
> What will survive of us is love.

Chichester Cathedral is open every day of the year, free of charge. Guided tours are available and there is a special trail for children. Groups are able to book a range of tours, including the 'Behind the Scenes' tour, which takes them up spiral staircases to the private Cathedral Library and Song School. The superb Cloisters Café and shop offer visitors a terrace and walled garden and, even on rainy days, visitors can gaze at the cathedral's spectacular spire through the café's glazed roof. The beautiful, secluded Bishop's Palace Gardens are just a short walk away behind the cathedral.

The cathedral boasts a vibrant calendar of events, many free of charge, including exhibitions, talks, lectures and lunchtime and evening concerts. The daily services underpin cathedral life, as has been the case throughout the centuries. This welcoming cathedral is home to both regular and occasional worshippers, visitors of any faith and those with no faith – a fascinating place to visit.

BISHOP'S PALACE GARDENS

Adjacent to the Cathedral, set against a backdrop of the Roman walls, Bishop's Palace Gardens are a hidden oasis located in the centre of the city. They make a perfect summer picnic spot, where you can enjoy the beautiful flora against the backdrop of Roman bastions.

CHICHESTER MARKET CROSS

Standing proudly in the centre of Chichester, the Cross is a local landmark, much loved as a meeting place and providing a convenient centre point from which to navigate your way around the city. The finest and most elaborate surviving structure of its kind in England, it was given to the city by Edward Storey (Bishop of Chichester 1478–1503) to provide shelter for people coming in from the countryside to sell their produce without paying a toll.

The Cross is an eight-sided structure made of Caen stone and has a central column which is supported by eight flying buttresses. Around the base of the column is a low stone seating area. Each side of the Cross has an arch carved with a bishop's mitre or headdress and bosses of demi-angels. On four sides of the Cross you can see tablets commemorating repairs made in the reign of Charles II.

THE PREBENDAL SCHOOL

The Prebendal School is a unique part of Chichester life and is the oldest school in Sussex, probably dating back to the foundation of the cathedral. The Prebendal's historic buildings on West Street blend perfectly with its modern and forward-thinking curriculum. It was refounded in 1497 by Bishop Edward Storey, who attached it to the Prebend of Highleigh in Chichester Cathedral and thus gave the School its present name.

   The charming 13th-century school house, with its historic narrow tower, still stands in West Street. Long Dorm, on the top floor, contains 300-year-old panelling and three adjoining 18th-century houses have been added. Over the years, the school has developed further extensions and also uses part of the Bishop's Palace next to the main school buildings.

The school is not open to the general public.

- The Prebendal School possesses a papal bull from 1253 (the time of St Richard).
- The early Jacobean panelling of the old schoolhouse, crowded with the carved names of pupils, is in the School's Long Dorm.
- King Henry VIII had been tutored by Prebendal head master, John Holt.
- The Prebendal began as a 'Song School', housing and teaching the Choristers – a tradition that continues today.

   Today, the Prebendal School is a thriving independent co-educational preparatory school for children aged 3–13 years, with small classes, high academic achievement and scholarship success. It has an unrivalled reputation for music and the cathedral choristers are educated at the school. Sport also plays a major part, as does the school's bespoke personal development programme. Every child has the opportunity to learn camp craft and take part in initiative-building exercises, and the school's official Beach School status allows the younger pupils to enjoy learning beyond the classroom.

North Street

As you head up North Street, a few metres from the Market Cross, you will pass St Olave's Church on your right. Now used as a bookshop, occasional services are still held here. Built in around 1050, this ancient church is in parts older than the cathedral, and has Roman building material within its walls. It is believed to be dedicated to Olaf II Haraldsson, patron saint of Norway, who came to England in 1013. The church may have been built by Scandinavian merchants.

THE COUNCIL HOUSE

Further up North Street, again on the right, you will pass the home of the Chichester City Council. The Council House is a group of connected buildings built between 1731 and 1881. The frontage is Palladian in style and at the top of the façade, under the lion, is a Latin inscription which translates as follows:

In order that the Council and the people of Chichester and their prosperity might be happy and fortunate this Council House was begun and completed in the year of our Lord 1731 in the reign of George II, Elector and King.

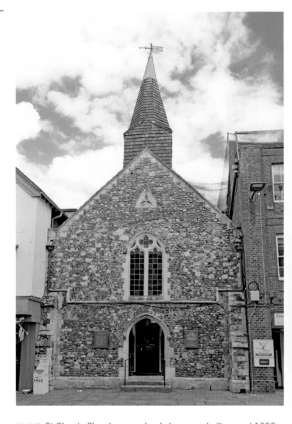

ABOVE St Olave's Church, now a bookshop, was built around 1050 and still contains Roman building materials

DEDICATION TO NEPTUNE AND MINERVA

To the left of the Council House entrance is a Roman stone inscription discovered in the immediate area in 1723. It is believed to have come from a Roman temple dedicated to Neptune and Minerva which was previously sited here.

CITY OF CHICHESTER CREST

The City Council's coat of arms was granted by Royal Patent in 1570 and is officially described as 'Argent gutte-de-sang, on a chief gules a lion passant guardant' or more simply 'silver with red drops, a straight line not indented, with leopard of England'.

LEFT The Council House, with Palladian frontage

INSET Chichester City Council's coat of arms

ABOVE 'Murray or none'. A painting of Admiral Sir George Murray in 1815

ABOVE The Ship Hotel, built for Admiral Sir George Murray in 1804

INDENT Murray's blue plaque, commemorating his importance to Admiral Lord Nelson

THE CHICHESTER HARBOUR HOTEL
(Formally The Ship Hotel)

Continue up North Street and you will arrive at The Chichester Harbour Hotel, the private home of Admiral Sir George Murray. This fine Georgian edifice was built in 1804. The grand new Georgian house became known as 'The Admiralty' due to its spacious rooms and in recognition of the owner's profession. It is still possible to imagine the house as Murray would have known it, particularly when gazing on the grand sweeping staircase.

Born in Chichester, Murray was a close friend of Admiral Nelson and one of his captains at the battle of Copenhagen. In 1805, Murray's influential father-in-law Lieutenant Colonel Teesdale died and Murray was named the executor of his complex will. This meant Murray was left behind to settle his affairs while Nelson went back to sea on HMS *Victory*. Feeling he could find no adequate substitute, Nelson left the Captain of the Fleet post

vacant. It was a case of 'Murray or none'! Murray therefore missed the Battle of Trafalgar, in which his great friend Nelson was killed. Murray became Mayor of Chichester on 25 September 1815 and died in this house in 1819, most likely from a heart attack, aged 59. He and his wife, Ann, are buried in Chichester Cathedral.

During the Second World War General Eisenhower, Supreme Allied Commander, stayed here on the eve of the D-Day landings in France in June 1944.

PRIORY PARK

Follow Guildhall Street around to the right just before the Chichester Harbour Hotel and you will see the gates of the beautiful Priory Park. Steeped in history, the park became a subscriber's park in the mid-19th century, when it was owned by the Duke of Richmond. It was presented to the City of Chichester Council by the Duke in 1918.

Priory Park is the setting for three scheduled monuments: the Guildhall, the remaining mound of Chichester Castle and the Roman city walls to the north and east.

THE GUILDHALL

The stunning Guildhall boasts a long and eventful history. Between 1269 and 1283 it was originally built as a Franciscan friary. Believed to have been the chancel of the friary, it contained the high altar and would only have been used by the resident Greyfriars, who remained in Priory Park for more than two centuries until the dissolution of monasteries in the 16th Century.

In 1538 the friary was closed under the orders of King Henry VIII. With the exception of the chancel, all buildings belonging to the friary were demolished. The site was then given to the Mayor of Chichester.

In 1541 the City Corporation bought the chancel from the Mayor of Chichester. The building was used as law courts and the Town Hall, or Guildhall. During this time some famous trials were held here, including those of the Hawkhurst Gang of smugglers in 1749, and the poet and artist William Blake in 1804.

In 1850 the building was no longer used as a Guildhall, instead becoming an armoury and drill

ABOVE The Guildhall has had many uses over the centuries and is now used for weddings and exhibitions

BELOW An artist's impression of the friary in around 1300, by Mike Codd.

hall for the Sussex Rifle Volunteers. In 1947 the building was briefly opened up for an exhibition of artefacts showcasing Chichester's history. In 2015 the Guildhall was granted a wedding licence and was used as a wedding venue for the first time in its history.

CHICHESTER CASTLE

Soon after the Norman Invasion, Earl Roger de Montgomerie ordered the construction of a motte-and-bailey castle. It was built in the north-east corner of the city, partially enclosed by the city wall, and probably required the destruction of several properties already there.

Today, the remains of the raised mound (motte) are still visible in Priory Park. The keep was constructed from timber. Some castles were later rebuilt in stone, but there is no evidence for this having taken place in Chichester.

In 1192, when King Richard was captured in Austria, we know that the castle was well stocked with barley, beans and bacon. This was probably in anticipation of a siege by the forces of Prince John, the King's brother. In 1216 the castle briefly surrendered to the French, but the following spring it was recaptured by the English, who demolished it to its foundations on the orders of King Henry III.

Between 1222 and 1269 the site of the castle was given by Richard, brother of King Henry, to the Franciscan Friars to build a new friary.

ABOVE The mound where the motte-and-bailey castle once stood

BELOW The motte and bailey of Chichester Castle, on the site of what is now Priory Park, by Mike Codd

ABOVE Chichester Festival Theatre and the Minerva Theatre. The Festival Theatre opened in 1962 and remains a flagship theatre

CHICHESTER FESTIVAL THEATRE

Head back to North Street and continue along the road out of the city centre until you reach an underpass on the right-hand side. Take the underpass and make your way through the car park, where in the distance you will see the world famous Chichester Festival Theatre.

Founded by a local ophthalmic optician and former city mayor, Leslie Evershed-Martin, the building follows an idea he had whilst watching a television programme in 1959 about the Tyrone Guthrie Theatre Festival in Stratford Ontario, Canada. Working tirelessly with Chichester City Council for support and to find a suitable site, he motivated local individuals and businesses to raise the £105,000 needed to make his idea a reality.

Following the Stratford model, the architects, Philip Powell and Hidalgo Moya, developed a theatre that arranged the auditorium around a stage that thrust itself into the centre of the audience, combining ancient Greek and Roman precedents with elements of Elizabethan theatre. When Chichester Festival Theatre opened in 1962, it was Britain's first modern thrust stage theatre.

ABOVE Chichester Festival Theatre and surrounding gardens and picnic area.

Between 1962 and 1965, the first artistic director Laurence Olivier established a company of actors and other theatre practitioners at Chichester Festival Theatre, who became the nucleus of his National Theatre Company. Today, Chichester Festival Theatre is one of the UK's flagship theatres, renowned for the exceptionally high standard of its productions, which feature many of the country's finest actors, directors and playwrights, as well as its work with the community and young people. Productions frequently transfer to the West End or tour internationally. The annual summer Festival season runs from April to October; year-round programming continues through the winter with the top quality touring productions.

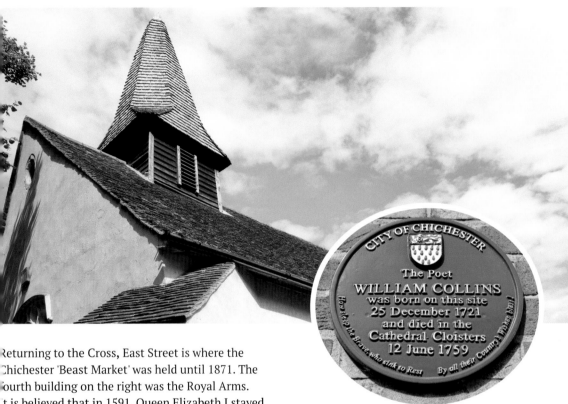

Returning to the Cross, East Street is where the Chichester 'Beast Market' was held until 1871. The fourth building on the right was the Royal Arms. It is believed that in 1591, Queen Elizabeth I stayed here when the building belonged to Alderman William Holland.

This bustling and popular shopping street will lead you to the Oxmarket and the Pallants, as well as the façade of the former Shippams factory and the *Symbol of Discovery*.

OXMARKET

Continuing along East Street, shortly after St Martin's Street, you will discover a small alleyway. This leads to St Andrew's Oxmarket. This Grade II listed medieval church is now the home of the Oxmarket Centre of Arts. It was mostly built in the 13th Century and is deconsecrated. The poet William Collins is buried here and you will see a plaque in commemoration. The remains of a Roman tessellated pavement were discovered underneath the church prior to restoration works carried out before its conversion into an arts centre in the 1970s.

The Oxmarket Centre of Arts is a volunteer run charity with a primary mission to promote and support local art and artists in a professional and inclusive manner.

THE PALLANTS

Directly opposite St Martin's Street is North Pallant. The four Pallants, mimicking the plan of the city, are also laid out in the form of a cross. They represent classic examples of Georgian architecture, with most of the houses dating from the 18th century. A few of the buildings are much older and have had new frontages added over the years.

Until 1846, the Archbishop of Canterbury had the exclusive jurisdiction (the Palantine) over this area of Chichester. 'Palantine' is derived from the Latin 'Palantia' which has been further corrupted to 'the Pallants'.

PALLANT HOUSE GALLERY

Walking down North Pallant, you will find Pallant House Gallery on the left. It is a Grade I listed building and one of the finest examples of a Queen Anne house in the country. Two stone birds that appear to be dodos guard the front entrance. It is believed that local wine merchant Henry Peckham, the owner of the house, requested ostriches (which feature in the Peckham family crest) when he commissioned the work, but the sculptor had never seen such birds and the result is the carvings you see today. The house is sometimes known locally as 'Dodo house'.

Today, Pallant House Gallery is a remarkable hybrid, with the old townhouse now adjoined by an award-winning contemporary wing. They opened to the public together as Pallant House Gallery in 2006.

Pallant House first opened as a public gallery of modern art in 1982 when the then Dean of Chichester Cathedral, Walter Hussey (1909-85) offered his private collection of modern British art – including works by John Piper, Ceri Richards and Graham Sutherland – to the city of Chichester on the condition that it was displayed in Pallant House.

TOP Pallant House, with its famous dodos, is one of the finest Queen Anne townhouses in the country

RIGHT One of the stone dodos adorning the gates of Pallant House

FAR RIGHT The intersection of the Pallants, which mimic the layout of the city centre

WEST PALLANT

ABOVE John Skelton's 1963 sculpture, *Symbol of Discovery*, received Grade II listed status in 2016

SYMBOL OF DISCOVERY

Continue down East Street and you will come to a street called Little London on your left. As the street bends right, on the corner of East Row, you will find the statue *Symbol of Discovery* in front of the site of the old Chichester District Museum. The Grade II listed statue dates from 1963 and was created by sculptor John Skelton (1923-1999) who was a nephew of Eric Gill. The sculpture depicts two hands cradling a man-made jewel of gold leaf set in plastic. It was commissioned by Stanley Roth, a local architect.

SHIPPAM'S

Further down East Street look out for the giant wishbone symbol of Shippam's on your left, a reminder of the successful family-run company, famous for their jars of fish and meat paste. Shippam's was founded in Chichester in the 18th century. The family were prominent grocers and, later, butchers in the town. In 1892, they expanded by building a factory behind the butcher's shop to manufacture canned goods and potted meats. Almost every household in the country enjoyed Shippam's paste for their tea. At their heyday in the 1950s the number of jars sold annually reached 43 million.

TOP The iconic Shippam's clock and wishbone symbol still hang from the building's façade

ABOVE Workers from the successful family-run Shippam's factory in 1909

RIGHT A 1937 advert for Shippam's highly popular meat and fish pastes

17

South Street

CANON GATE

Heading down South Street from the Cross you will pass the historic Canon Gate and the street will eventually lead you past the Chichester Combined Court and Family Court Hearing Centre, the railway station and down to the Chichester Canal Basin.

Canon Gate is a Grade I listed building dating to the 16th century. The special court of Pie Powder (*pieds poussiéreux* or 'dusty feet') was held in the upper chamber of Canongate over the archway. This court was held during the annual Sloe Fair to resolve any disputes which may have arisen.

The Sloe Fair dates back to the 12th century and is still held annually in Chichester in October. The right to hold the fair was granted by Henry I to Bishop Luffa in 1107. It became known as the Sloe Fair because it was held in a field just outside the North Gate, where it was said a sloe tree laden with fruit was growing. The manorial court of the Bishop's Manor of Canon Gate was also held here. At one time the space between the small arches was used as a stable, but this was removed when the building was renovated in 1894.

TOP The 16th-century Canon Gate from South Street, with a view of the magnificent cathedral spire.

ABOVE Looking back into South Street from Canon Lane and the Cathedral Precincts

CHICHESTER CANAL BASIN

Continue down South Street and across the railway line past the station. On the left you will come to the 'green lung' of Chichester, the charming Chichester Canal Basin.

The Chichester Ship Canal is a leisure waterway linking historic Chichester to the sea. The canal runs four miles from the Basin to the Harbour at Birdham and, today, the two miles as far as Donnington remain navigable.

It is valued by local residents and holidaymakers who enjoy the many activities – narrow boat trips, rowing, canoeing, rambling, fishing, and cycling.

Although known today as the Chichester Canal, it is in fact part of the former Portsmouth and Arundel Canal. This was opened in 1823 and consisted of a 12-mile canal from Ford on the River Arun to the Salterns, and a shorter cut from Langstone Harbour to Portsmouth Harbour, connected together by a 13-mile dredged 'bargeway' through the natural harbours and channels between them.

Intended as a key link in a through route to London via the River Arun Navigation, Wey and Arun Junction Canal, River Wey and River Thames, it was not a success. By the time it was built, there was no real need for an inland route as larger and better ships, coupled with an end to hostilities with France, meant that the coastal route was an easier and cheaper option.

One of the few regular through cargoes carried was gold bullion from Portsmouth to the Bank of England, with armed guards on the barges.

RIGHT A tranquil view of the Chichester Ship Canal as it leaves the Basin, along with its resident swans

BELOW Narrowboat trips are available from the Canal Basin, with rowing boats available for those feeling more athletic

Roman Chichester

The earliest evidence for Roman settlement was in the form of timber buildings. Following the death of Togidubnus and the establishment of complete Roman control, major investment led to the construction of stone buildings and the creation of an infrastructure associated with all the elements of Roman culture and society, including public baths, the forum basilica, temples, roads and an amphitheatre. The city walls were constructed in the late 3rd century AD, enclosing the centre of the town and comprised of earth banks fronted with a stone-faced wall and a large ditch. By the middle of the 4th century AD, semi-circular towers (bastions) had been added, which were capable of housing siege artillery.

To find out more about Roman Chichester, visit The Novium Museum and take a stroll around the City Walls Walk, signposted around the city.

ROMAN CHICHESTER – NOVIOMAGUS REGINORUM

Chichester was first established by the Romans as the town of Noviomagvs Reginorvm, which translates as 'new market of proud people'.

After the conquest the local tribe, known as the Regini were led by a native ruler Tiberius Claudius Togidubnus, who was one of the principal British supporters of the Romans. It was under Togidubnus that the first town on the site of Chichester was laid out as the tribal capital, the most important Roman centre in this part of the south-east.

The new town developed in association with a major road, now known as Stane Street, which ran between Chichester and London.

PREVIOUS PAGE
ABOVE The original name of the city was Noviomagus Reginorum

PREVIOUS PAGE
BELOW The Roman walls are still largely intact

LEFT View to Canon's Lane from the south entrance to Chichester Cathedral

BELOW Roman re-enactors outside the Novium Museum

Around Chichester

Directly surrounding Chichester you will find the rolling South Downs to the north and picturesque coastline to the south. There is a wide variety of places to discover, rich in history, art and architecture, including stunning gardens, historic houses, museums and theatre.

Fishbourne Roman Palace

Roman Way, Fishbourne,
Chichester PO19 3QR
T: 01243 785859
www.sussexpast.co.uk

Since the site was discovered in 1960, visitors to Fishbourne Roman Palace have been able to view the largest collection of early Roman mosaic floors in Britain. The museum displays artefacts found during the excavations, including beautiful jewellery and personal items. The formal garden is laid out to its original plan, featuring box hedging and staked espalier fruit trees with a plants garden showcasing many culinary and medicinal plants available during the life of the Palace. Visitors are invited to take a view behind the scenes in the Collections Discovery Centre which houses over a million artefacts in the bulk and sensitive stores.

Tangmere Military Aviation Museum

Gamecock Terrace, Tangmere,
Nr Chichester PO20 2ES
T: 01243 790090
www.tangmere-museum.org.uk

Tangmere Military Aviation Museum is situated in a corner of the old RAF Tangmere airfield, famed for its illustrious service from 1916 through to the post-war years. It was opened by a group of aviation enthusiasts in 1982 to 'promote public awareness of the UK's military aviation heritage, educate present and future generations in military aviation and serve as a memorial to airmen and airwomen who gave their lives in the service of this country'.

The museum is home to an impressive display of historic aircraft and a unique collection of aviation memorabilia stretching from the First World War through to the Cold War. Amongst the many attractions are numerous interactive displays and several aircraft simulators for visitors to experience. There is something for all members of the family to see and do.

The South Downs Planetarium and Science Centre

Kingsham Road,
Chichester PO19 8AE
T: 01243 774400
www.southdowns.org.uk

At the Planetarium you can see the stars at any time – even in broad daylight! Whilst sitting comfortably you can see the night sky and nearly 4,500 stars and planets that the star projector displays on the domed ceiling of the star theatre, with no interference from weather or bright lights. The South Downs Planetarium is a registered educational charity run almost entirely by a dedicated team of nearly 60 volunteers and astronomy enthusiasts who give their time and knowledge to make a visit to the Planetarium a marvellous experience for people of all ages from six years upwards.

Since the planetarium was opened by the Astronomer Royal, Lord Rees, in 2001, it has welcomed more than 200,000 visitors.

Operating year-round, the Planetarium is largely occupied with visits from schools in term time. During the evenings, weekends and school holidays there is a regular programme of more than 100 shows a year when it is open to the public. Details are available on the Planetarium website and tickets are sold at the Tourist Information Centre. It is only open to the public at other times when there is a show, so give them a call before you visit.

Cass Sculpture Foundation

Open Air Museum & Gardens
Cass Sculpture Foundation
New Barn Hill,
Goodwood PO18 0QP
01243 538449
www.sculpture.org.uk

Cass Sculpture Foundation is a charity that was founded in order to provide patronage to artists at an organisational level. Set within 26 acres of magical woodland on the Goodwood Estate, it is home to an evolving display that has included sculptures by Jake and Dinos Chapman, Rachel Whiteread, Tony Cragg, and Sara Barker amongst others. Cass has been commissioning artists to realise large-scale sculptures since 1992. Artists are invited to submit proposals in the form of a maquette and work on paper. Once an artist is selected, Cass offers support and expertise at every stage of the process, from conception to fabrication exhibition to sale. All the works on display are available for sale, with proceeds channelled directly into future opportunities for artists.

West Dean Gardens

West Dean,
Chichester PO18 0RX
T: 01243 818210
www.westdean.org.uk/gardens

Nestled at the foot of the South Downs just six miles north of Chichester, West Dean Gardens is one of the greatest restored English gardens open to the public today. Escape to the glorious gardens and parkland to explore a wide range of features including the 13 Victorian glasshouses housing orchids, fuchsias, figs, vines, melons and chillies, the Walled Kitchen Garden of classic Victorian design, the 300-foot Edwardian Pergola designed by Harold Peto, the naturalistic Spring Garden, the award-winning Sunken Garden and the orchards. The circular 2.5 mile St Roche's Arboretum walk, set in 49 acres of beautiful parkland, offers spectacular panoramic views of the South Downs.

Enjoy lunch or afternoon tea in the gardens restaurant (and breakfast at weekends and on bank holidays), and browse the gardens shop for unique gifts and plants. Dogs on a short lead are welcome. West Dean Gardens and College hold a variety of events throughout the year – an Arts & Craft Festival including the Annual House Opening, the Chilli Fiesta, plus special family-friendly activities for special occasions such as Mother's Day, Easter, Halloween, the Apple Fair and, of course, visit Father Christmas.

Weald & Downland Living Museum

Town Lane, Singleton,
Chichester PO18 0EU
T: 01243 811363
www.wealddown.co.uk

At this wonderful museum you can discover 50 traditional buildings in a 40-acre rural landscape, which tell the stories of the people who lived and worked in them over a 600-year period. Many buildings feature recreated historic interiors and there is a regular programme of demonstrations.

STATELY HOMES

Goodwood House

Kennel Hill, Goodwood,
Chichester, PO18 0PX
T: 01243 755000
www.goodwood.com

Goodwood House is the family seat of the Dukes of Richmond. It is set in the heart of the Sussex Downs and houses astonishing treasures, including celebrated paintings by George Stubbs and Canaletto, fine furniture, Gobelin Tapestries and Sevres porcelain.

Stansted Park

Rowland's Castle,
Hampshire PO9 6DX
T: 02392 412265
www.stanstedpark.co.uk

Set in 1800 acres of ancient forest, Stansted Park is a fascinating and fun day out for the whole family. Inside the mansion house you will find an unrivalled upstairs/downstairs experience, with magnificent state rooms and extensive servants' quarters. Around the estate you can ride the little train through the arboretum, or visit the many other attractions, including the unique private chapel, stunning new farm shop, children's play area and maze.

Petworth House

Church Street, Petworth,
West Sussex GU28 0AE
T: 01798 342207
www.nationaltrust.org.uk/
petworth-house-and-park

Located in the South Downs National Park, Petworth is known as an impressive mansion surrounded by a 700-acre deer park landscaped by Capability Brown. The state rooms within the mansion display the finest collection of art in the care of the National Trust, including works by Turner, Reynolds, Blake and Van Dyck. Separate Servants' Quarters offer a glimpse of life 'below stairs', featuring domestic rooms and the Historic Kitchen with a 1000-piece copper *batterie de cuisine*. The palatial mansion was built in 1682 when heiress, Elizabeth Percy, daughter to the 11th Earl of Northumberland, married Charles Seymour, 6th Duke of Somerset.The state rooms are saturated with internationally important paintings by artists such as Van Dyck, Reynolds, Titian and Blake together with classical and neo-classical sculptures. Follow in the footsteps of JMW Turner, who spent long periods at the mansion under the patronage of the 3rd Earl of Egremont, and whose paintings of Petworth Park can be seen in the Carved Room today.

Uppark House & Garden

South Harting,
Petersfield, GU31 5QR
T: 01730 825415
www.nationaltrust.org.uk/uppark

Perched on its vantage point high on the South Downs ridge, Uppark commands views as far south as the English Channel. Outside, the intimate gardens are being gradually restored to their original 18th-century design, with plenty of space in the adjacent meadow to play and relax with a picnic. The nearby woodland is great for exploring and den-building.

Uppark's Georgian interiors illustrate the comfort of life 'upstairs', in contrast with the 'downstairs' world of the servants. A highlight of the collection is one of the best examples of a 17th-century doll's house in the country.

Due to its high elevation, Uppark is exposed to extremes of weather, particularly in the winter months. This can lead to closure of the property at short notice. To avoid disappointment please call to check that Uppark is open before setting out.

COAST AND HARBOUR

Chichester Harbour Water Tours

T: 01243 670504
www.chichesterharbourwatertours.co.uk

Chichester Harbour is one of the county's hidden treasures. One of only a few undeveloped estuaries on the South Coast, the natural harbour is 22 square miles of low-lying land and water. On the border of Hampshire and West Sussex, and set against a backdrop of the South Downs, the area was declared an Area of Outstanding Beauty in 1964, and it is easy to see why. The landscape has remained relatively wild and unspoilt, making it rich in wildlife. It has the sixth largest area of saltmarsh in Britain, along with other important habitats such as sand dunes, vegetated shingle, saline lagoons, ancient woodland and coastal grazing marsh. In recognition of this unique environment and its important for both national and international conservation, the area is a designated Site of Special Scientific Interest.

Chichester Harbour is also a haven for sailors and is one of Britain's most popular stretches of water for boating. The waters are home to 14 sailing clubs and as many as 12,500 vessels regularly use the waters for sport and leisure. This popularity dates right back to the Roman period when the harbour was initially developed as a military base. As Chichester grew and developed, the palace at Fishbourne was built, the harbour became integral to the local community and soon a network of roads began to spread from the area, leading right up to London. Stane Street – the Roman artery from Chichester to London – began at Dell Quay.

The excellent wetlands and stunning coastline have been a magnet for both residents and tourists alike for centuries and there is still evidence of the early Saxon settlers. In the saltings many examples of broken dykes show where landowners attempted to reclaim land from marsh. Over the centuries agriculture flourished and the harbour developed as an important port for grain, with landings at Dell Quay, Bosham and, from the 13th century onwards, Emsworth. The harbour never had deep-water anchorages but it served coastal trading until well after the arrival of the railways. There were considerable fishing fleets and a flourishing oyster dredging industry until well into the 20th century.

Boat tours of the Harbour offer further insight into the fascinating history of Chichester Harbour. They run regularly in the summer season.

West Wittering Beach

Pound Road, West Wittering,
Chichester PO20 8AJ
T: 01243 514143
www.westwitteringbeach.co.uk

Set on the edge of Chichester Harbour is West Wittering, a large stretch of pristine, unspoilt sandy beach. The area is perfect for a family day out, picnic or stroll along the sand dunes with a spectacular view of the sunset. The windy conditions and sheltered waters make it a Mecca for all watersports enthusiasts, especially wind surfers and kiteboarders. Shallow lagoons and extensive sandy beaches are revealed at low tide. The area is internationally recognised for its wildlife, birds, highest water quality and unique beauty. It's no surprise that it is one of the premier Blue Flag beaches in the country. There is a fee for using the car park directly adjoining the beach.

Dogs are welcome on the site.

Information

Chichester Tourist Information Centre
The Novium Museum, Tower Street,
Chichester, West Sussex, P019 1QH
Tel: 01243 775888
Email: chitic@chichester.gov.uk
Website: www.thenovium.org

CHICHESTER & DISTRICT ATTRACTIONS

Bignor Roman Villa
01798 869259
www.bignorromanvilla.co.uk

Cass Sculpture Park
01243 538449
www.sculpture.org.uk

Chichester Canal Trust
01243 771363
www.chichestercanal.org.uk

Chichester Cathedral
01243 782595
www.chichestercathedral.org.uk

Chichester Festival Theatre
01243 781312
www.cft.org.uk

Chichester Harbour Conservancy
01243 512301
www.conservancy.co.uk

Fishbourne Roman Palace
01243 785859
www.sussexpast.co.uk

Goodwood House
01243 755040
www.goodwood.com

Oxmarket Gallery
01243 779103
www.oxmarket.com

Pallant House Gallery
01243 774557
www.pallant.org.uk

Petworth House & Park
01798 342207
www.nationaltrust.org.uk/petworth-house

South Downs Planetarium
01243 774400
www.southdowns.org.uk

Stansted Park
02392 412265
www.stanstedpark.co.uk

Tangmere Military Avaition Museum
01243 790090
www.tangmere-museum.org.uk

Uppark House & Garden
01730 825415
www.nationaltrust.org.uk/uppark

Weald & Downland Living Museum
01243 811348
www.wealddown.co.uk

West Dean Gardens
01243 818210
www.westdean.org.uk

West Wittering Beach
01243 514143
www.westwitteringbeach.co.uk

South Downs national Park Authority
01730 814810
www.southdowns.gov.uk

TOURS & TRIPS

Chichester Harbour Tours
01243 670504
www.chichesterharbourwatertours.co.uk

Chichester City Tours
01243 775888
www.chicitytours.co.uk

Chichester Tour Guides
01243 850533
www.chtg.co.uk